ANACONDAS

by Jaclyn Jaycox

PEBBLE
a capstone imprint

Pebble Explore is published by Pebble, an imprint of Capstone.
1710 Roe Crest Drive
North Mankato, Minnesota 56003
www.capstonepub.com

Library of Congress Cataloging-in-Publication Data is available on the Library of Congress website.
ISBN: 978-1-9771-1340-5 (library binding)
ISBN: 978-1-9771-1793-9 (paperback)
ISBN: 978-1-9771-1348-1 (eBook PDF)

Summary: Simple text and photographs present anacondas, their body parts, and behavior.

Photo Credits
Associated Press: Gemunu Amarasinghe, 25; Getty Images: Sylvain CORDIER, 23; Minden Pictures: Franco Banfi, 15, Mark Bowler, 18, Tony Crocetta, 17; Newscom: Danita Delimont Photography, 9, E. Hummel, 27, Martin Wendler/NHPA/Photoshot, 19, Michael S. Nolan, 7, Morales/agefotostock, 22, TUNS/picture alliance / Arco Images G, 5; Shutterstock: Frank Cornelissen, 1, Michael Meshcheryakov, 13, nounours, 12, Uwe Bergwitz, Cover, Vadim Petrakov, 8, Vladimir Wrangel, 11, wayak, 21, worldclassphoto, 14

Editorial Credits
Hank Musolf, editor; Dina Her, designer; Morgan Walters, media researcher; Tori Abraham, production specialist

Printed and bound in China.
002489

Table of Contents

Words in **bold** are in the glossary.

Amazing Anacondas

What is green, has no legs, and is as long as a bus? A green anaconda! These snakes spend time in rivers waiting for food. They are huge. They can eat animals as big as cows whole!

Anacondas are a type of **reptile**. They can't control their body heat. If it's cold outside, they are cold. If it's hot outside, they are hot. There are four kinds of these snakes. They are the green, yellow, dark-spotted, and Bolivian anacondas.

Where in the World

Anacondas live in **rain forests** in South America. These forests are in **tropical** areas. They get a lot of rain. These snakes are great swimmers. They spend most of their time in water. They live in swamps and rivers.

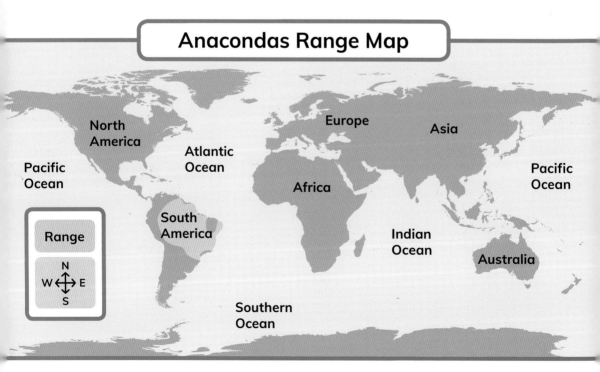

Anacondas Range Map

North America

Europe

Asia

Atlantic Ocean

Pacific Ocean

Africa

Pacific Ocean

Range

South America

Indian Ocean

Australia

N
W E
S

Southern Ocean

Anacondas can also move on land. They live in grasslands. They climb trees. They hang from the branches to dry off. They also rest in empty holes called **burrows**.

Spotted Snakes

The green anaconda is well known. It is the heaviest snake. It is also one of the longest. These snakes can weigh more than 550 pounds (250 kilograms). That's as much as a lion! They grow up to 30 feet (9 meters) long. Females are usually much larger than males.

green anaconda

yellow anaconda

The yellow, dark-spotted, and
Bolivian anacondas are smaller. They
grow to be about 9 feet (2.7 m) long.

Green anacondas are dark green. Other types can be brown or yellow. They have black or brown spots. They blend in with the rivers. They can hide in rain forests. Doing this protects them from animals that hunt them. It makes the snakes hard to see.

scales

Anacondas have thick bodies. Like most other reptiles, anacondas have hard pieces of skin on their bodies. They are called **scales.** Their eyes and nostrils are on top of their heads. This helps them hunt. They can keep their heads above the water. They look for animals to eat.

These snakes have sharp teeth. Their jaws are stretchy. They can swallow big animals. They can eat ones much bigger than their heads!

On the Menu

Anacondas can eat a lot. They eat birds, mice, fish, turtles, and other **prey**. They also eat animals such as pigs, deer, and even jaguars. Females might even eat small male anacondas!

These snakes are **nocturnal**. They sleep during the day. They hunt at night. They hunt in the water more than on land. They don't move as well on land.

Anacondas don't chase their prey. They wait for it to come near. They grab their prey. They bite the animal. They hold it with their powerful jaws. Then they wrap around the prey. They squeeze. The animal can't breathe, and it dies.

Anacondas swallow their prey whole. They have stretchy bodies. They change shape to fit their meals. It can take a week to break down a meal. They can go a long time without eating again. They can go weeks or months.

If the snakes face danger after a meal, they throw up. Having a big animal inside them causes them to move slower. They throw up to make a quick getaway.

Life of an Anaconda

Anacondas live alone. They have their own hunting areas. They don't usually cross paths. They only come together to **mate**.

Mating season is from April to May. Females leave a **scent** to attract males. Males will travel far to find to a female. Their tongues help them find their way. They can pick up the female's smell with their tongues.

Females carry their babies for about seven months. They do not hunt during this time. They also don't eat. The mother gives birth to live babies. They have about 30 at a time.

The baby snakes are about 2 feet (0.6 m) long. Their coloring is much like the adults. The mother doesn't care for the babies. She swims away from them right after they are born. The babies can swim and hunt on their own. They eat small mice, frogs, fish, and chicks.

Baby anacondas grow quickly. They can be 10 feet (3 m) long by age 3. They live about 10 years in the wild.

Threats to Anacondas

When anacondas are young, birds, wildcats, and other snakes may hunt them. They don't have many **predators** when they are grown. Humans are their biggest threat. They are hunted for their skin. People also catch them to sell as pets. This is against the law.

Some people are afraid of snakes. Anacondas are sometimes killed out of fear. People think the snakes will hurt them.

Habitat loss is also a threat. The rain forests are being cut down. Anaconda's homes are getting smaller.

There is a lot we don't know about anacondas. They are good at hiding. Scientists are studying them. Their work will help find better ways to protect the snakes. Many people try to help anacondas. They keep rivers clean. They make sure people don't cut down trees. This helps keep the snakes' homes safe.

Fast Facts

Name: anaconda

Habitat: rain forests, grasslands, swamps, marshes, rivers

Where in the World: South America

Food: birds, mice, fish, turtles, pigs, deer

Predators: humans, birds, wildcats, other snakes

Life span: 10 years

Glossary

burrow (BUHR-oh)—a tunnel or hole in the ground made or used by an animal

habitat (HAB-uh-tat)—the natural place or conditions in which a plant or animal lives

mate (MATE)—to join with another to produce young

nocturnal (nok-TUR-nuhl)—active at night and resting during the day

predator (PRED-uh-tur)—an animal that hunts other animals for food

prey (PRAY)—an animal hunted by another animal for food

rain forest (RAYN FOR-ist)—a forest where rain falls almost every day

reptile (REP-tile)—a cold-blooded animal that breathes air and has a backbone

scale (SKALE)—one of many small, hard pieces of skin that cover an animal's body

scent (SENT)—the smell of something

tropical (TRAH-pi-kuhl)—near the equator

Read More

Avery, Sebastian. *Anacondas*. New York: PowerKids Press, 2016.

Gagne, Tammy. *Snakes: Built for the Hunt*. North Mankato, Minn.: Capstone, 2016.

Lawrence, Ellen. *Green Anaconda*. New York: Bearport Publishing, 2017.

Internet Sites

Easy Science for Kids—All About Anacondas
easyscienceforkids.com/all-about-anacondas/

National Geographic Kids—Anacondas
kids.nationalgeographic.com/animals/
anaconda/#anaconda-swimming.jpg

San Diego Zoo Kids—Anaconda
kids.sandiegozoo.org/animals/anaconda

Index